DEVOTIONAL JOURNAL

MIRRORS IN MOTHERHOOD

KEONDRIA WALKER

To Emma, Zach, and Zoe
You are my greatest blessings and
my deepest inspiration. You are the
mirrors through which I see the purest
reflections of love, hope, and grace.
Each day with you unveils new lessons
in resilience and joy, reminding me
that Motherhood is not just a role,
but a journey of transformation,
unconditional love, and boundless
growth.
This book is a tribute to you, a testament
to the strength, faith, and devotion
that Motherhood has nurtured within
me. May you always walk in God's light,
knowing you are a precious gift, a reward
beyond measure.
With all my love,
Mom

CONTENTS

SECTION 4

The Power Of Prayer & Biblical Encouragement

SECTION 5

Healing, Growth, And Community In Motherhood

SECTION 6

Raising Godly Children

INTRODUCTION

Motherhood is one of the most beautiful yet challenging journeys a woman can embark on. It requires strength, patience, and unwavering love and faith, even when you feel exhausted, overwhelmed, or uncertain. As a mother, you must show up for your children, even when you are emotionally drained. You must press forward when you are weary, navigate through moments of anxiety, and find strength in times of self-doubt.

Mirrors in Motherhood aims to create a safe and stable sense of well-being for mothers of all backgrounds, pregnant moms, new moms, aspiring moms, adoptive moms, and every woman who has embraced the role of nurturing and protecting a child. Motherhood is not about perfection; but grace, growth, and leaning on God for guidance.

I was inspired to write this journal as I became a mother of three. Following my divorce and transitioning into single Motherhood, I had to rely on God to get me through and trust that he would give me the strength to raise my children, even though it was not an ideal situation. Through this journey, I learned that faith is the foundation of Motherhood, and with God's guidance, I found resilience, hope, and the ability to move forward with love.

This devotional journal is designed to support and uplift you by engaging in Godly principles and biblical truths to help you find balance amid the chaos. Through reflection, prayer, and intentional moments with God, Mirrors in Motherhood will encourage you to embrace the joys and challenges of Motherhood while deepening your faith. As you pour love into your children, may you also take the time to pour love into yourself, so that you can continue to be the mother God has called you to be.

Psalms 127:3

"Children are a gift from the Lord, they are a reward from him."

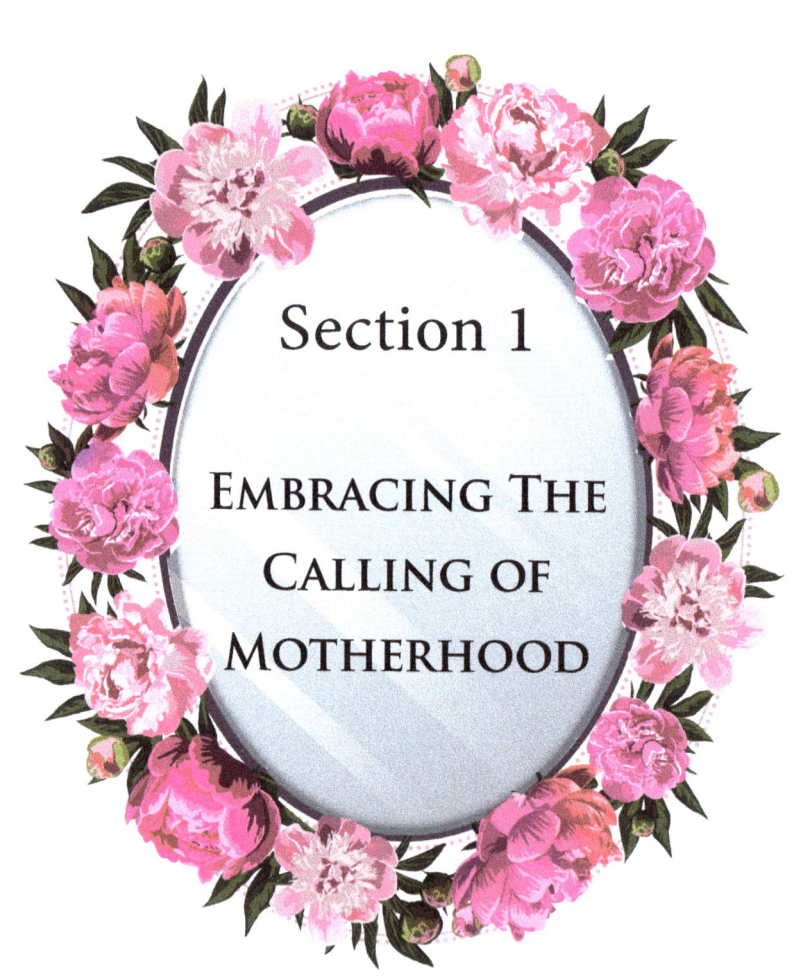

Section 1

EMBRACING THE
CALLING OF
MOTHERHOOD

THE ROOTS OF MOTHERHOOD

*"I am the vine; you are the branches. If you remain in
me and I in you, you will bear much fruit; apart from
me you can do nothing"*
John 15:5 NIV

The journey of life begins in infancy and unfolds into adulthood.
When God created humanity, He gave us the precious gift of life,
connecting us all through Him. This connection mirrors a tree, where
God is the trunk, the source of life, and we are the branches, drawing
strength and sustenance from Him.

Just as a tree's roots anchor it deeply into the soil, providing nourishment and stability, Motherhood is rooted in divine connection. When
we give birth, our children are physically connected to us through the
umbilical cord, a symbol of physical and emotional attachment. This
natural bond reflects a greater spiritual truth: we must remain deeply
connected to Jesus Christ as mothers. He is our spiritual nourishment,
the living water that strengthens our mind, body, and soul. Just as a
tree flourishes when firmly rooted, we can only thrive in our role as
mothers when we stay anchored in Him. When we draw from His
wisdom, patience, and love, we pass that same nourishment to our
children, allowing them to grow in faith and purpose (John 15:1-8).

Just as a tree thrives deeply rooted in rich soil, Motherhood flourishes
when grounded in God.

God as the Source (The Soil): Just as soil provides essential nutrients for a tree's survival, God is the foundation from which we, as

mothers, draw our strength, wisdom, and love. Staying connected to Him allows us to grow and bear fruit in our parenting journey.

Nourishment from God (The Nutrients): A tree absorbs nourishment from the soil to remain strong and healthy. Similarly, we must continuously seek spiritual nourishment—through prayer, scripture, and faith—to sustain ourselves and guide our children.

Mothers as the Branches (The Fruit): The branches stretch outward, bearing fruit and giving life. As mothers, we receive God's strength and extend His love to our children. Our connection to Him enables us to nurture, guide, and protect them.

The Mother-Child Connection (God's Love): Just as a branch remains connected to the tree, a mother shares a profound bond with her child. This physical and spiritual connection reflects God's love for us. When we remain deeply rooted in Him, we pass his teachings, wisdom, and grace to the next generation.

Reflection Questions:

1. In what ways do you feel spiritually nourished as a mother?

2. How can you deepen your connection with God to better guide your children?

3. What "fruit" are you producing in your motherhood journey?

FIRMLY PLANTED IN PRAYER

Heavenly Father,

Thank you for being the source of my strength, wisdom, and love. Like a tree planted by streams of water, I desire to be deeply rooted in you so that I may flourish as a mother. Lord, I acknowledge that apart from you, I can do nothing. Help me remain connected to you, drawing from your endless grace and truth. Nourish my soul, Father, so that I may pour patience, love, and wisdom into my children. When I feel weary, remind me that you are my refuge. When I feel uncertain, guide my steps. When I feel inadequate, cover me with your grace. Let my life reflect your love, teaching my children to walk in faith, trust in your Word, and find their purpose in you. May the fruit of my Motherhood glorify you, filled with kindness, faithfulness, and unwavering trust in your plan. Lord, just as the roots of a tree grow deeper with time, help me grow spiritually, anchoring myself in your truth so that no storm can shake me. Let my Motherhood be a testimony of your provision and love. I surrender my journey, children, and heart into your hands. Thank you for choosing me for this calling.

In Jesus' Name, Amen.

Reflecting God's Image

*"So God created mankind in his own image, in the
image of God he created them; male and female he
created them."*
Genesis 1:27 NIV

Our appearance does not define our worth or ability as mothers, yet
society often uses it as a tool to set unrealistic expectations. The world
associates Motherhood with exhaustion, unkept hair, and a loss of
identity, subtly suggesting that being a devoted mother means sacri-
ficing self-care. However, I see my appearance as a reflection of God's
image rather than the world's perception. When I align myself with
His presence, the beauty of God radiates from within, transforming
how I see myself and how others perceive me.

Motherhood can distort our sense of self, like a funhouse mirror that
alters reality. The transition into Motherhood irrevocably changes us
physically, emotionally, and spiritually, often challenging how we
view ourselves. The weight of daily responsibilities can sometimes
leave us feeling overwhelmed, bitter, or even disconnected from
the woman we once were. But when we see ourselves as vessels for
God, Motherhood becomes an act of worship rather than a burden.
Every sacrifice, every late night, and every moment of selflessness
is an offering to God.

While outward appearance has significance, it reflects God's creativ-
ity, true beauty is found in conforming to His image and likeness.
Our focus should not be on meeting worldly beauty standards but on
allowing His love, grace, and strength to shine through us. When our
hearts are rooted in Christ, His beauty becomes evident in everything

we do, from nurturing our children to carrying ourselves with confidence and dignity.

Reflection Activity: Seeing Yourself Through God's Eyes

We are mirrors, reflecting who God is to our children, families, and the world. Take a moment to answer the following questions:

1. How do I view myself as a mother? Is my perception based on God's truth or society's expectations?

2. In what ways do I reflect God's image in my daily life?

3. Are there areas where I struggle with self-image? How can I invite God into those insecurities?

4. How can I embrace Motherhood as an act of worship rather than a role of self-sacrifice alone?

As you reflect, don't be discouraged by any perceived shortcomings. Instead, ask yourself: How can I become Christ-like in my motherhood journey?

A Prayer for Reflecting God's Image in Motherhood

Heavenly Father,

Thank you for creating me in your image and entrusting me with the role of Motherhood. In a world that distorts beauty and value, help me to see myself through your eyes; worthy, loved, and fearfully made. When I feel weary, remind me that my strength comes from you. When I struggle with self-doubt, let your truth drown out the lies of comparison and unrealistic expectations. Lord, I desire to reflect your love, grace, and wisdom in my motherhood journey. Let my actions, words, and presence radiate your beauty; so my children see you in me. Help me embrace this calling confidently, knowing that my identity is not lost in Motherhood but refined through it. Please guide me to care for myself as your beloved daughter, understanding that self-care is not selfish but honoring the body and soul you have given me. Let me walk in the dignity and grace you have placed upon me, and may my children learn from my example what it means to be deeply rooted in your love. Lord, transform my insecurities into testimonies of your goodness. Shape me into the mother you have called me to be, one who leads with love, nurtures with wisdom, and reflects your image every season.

In Jesus' name, Amen.

THE PROVERBS 31 MOTHER

*"She is clothed with strength and dignity; she can laugh
at the days to come. She speaks with wisdom, and
faithful instruction is on her tongue."*
Proverbs 31:25-26 NIV

The Proverbs 31 woman is often seen as the ultimate example of godly
Motherhood, strong, wise, and full of kindness. But rather than being
an impossible standard, she inspires all mothers who seek to walk
in faith and grace.

EMBRACING WISDOM

Wisdom is more than knowledge; it is the ability to apply God's truth
in every season of life. A wise mother seeks God's guidance in raising
her children, knowing that her words and actions shape their future.
She does not rely solely on her understanding but trusts in the Lord
to lead her steps (Proverbs 3:5-6).

Ask yourself: Am I seeking God's wisdom in my parenting? Do my
words reflect His truth and love?

EMBRACING STRENGTH

Motherhood requires immense strength, not just physically, but
emotionally and spiritually. The Proverbs 31 mother is "clothed with
strength," meaning she finds her resilience in God. When challenges
arise, she does not crumble but stands firm in faith. True strength is
found in surrendering to God's power, knowing he upholds us when

we are weary (Isaiah 40:31).

Ask yourself: How do I find strength in God during difficult moments? Am I relying on His strength rather than my own?

EMBRACING KINDNESS

A mother's words and actions set the tone in her home. Proverbs 31:26 reminds us that "faithful instruction" is on her tongue, meaning she speaks life, encouragement, and correction with love. Her kindness is shown in what she says and how she serves her family. She reflects the character of Christ, who leads with love and compassion.

Ask yourself: Are my words building up or tearing down? How can I show more kindness and grace to my children and those around me?

A PRAYER FOR A PROVERBS 31 MOTHER

Heavenly Father,

Thank you for the example of the Proverbs 31 mother. Please help me to walk in wisdom, seeking your truth in every decision I make. Clothe me with strength, that I may face each day with faith and confidence in your plans. Fill my heart with kindness, so that my words and actions reflect your love. May my home be a place where your presence dwells, and may my children see you in me.

In Jesus' name, Amen.

Seasons of In Between

*"There is a time for everything, and a season for every
activity under the heavens."*
Ecclesiastes 3:1 NIV

Motherhood is a journey of seasons, filled with joy and laughter, others
with challenges and uncertainty. Sometimes, we feel confident in our
role, and others when we find ourselves in the "in-between" space
of waiting, growth, and transition. The newborn phase turns into
toddlerhood, childhood becomes adolescence, and before we know
it, we watch our children enter adulthood. In every shift, there is loss
and gain, letting go of one stage and embracing the next.

It is in these in-between moments that we often wrestle with uncertainty. Am I doing enough? Am I making the right decisions? What
comes next? Yet, God calls us to trust Him in the waiting. He reminds
us that every season has a purpose, and even in the unknown, He is
works all things for good (Romans 8:28).

When we find ourselves caught between what was and what is to come,
God offers us peace that surpasses all understanding (Philippians
4:7). Instead of fearing the next stage, we can rest in the knowledge
that God is guiding both us and our children. He is growing them
and refining us, teaching us patience, faith, and surrender. As our
children grow, we must learn to release control and trust that God
is leading their steps.

Instead of worrying about what's next, God invites us to be fully present
in our season. Each stage of parenting has its beauty, whether it's rock-
ing a baby to sleep, teaching a child to pray, or having heart-to-heart

conversations with a teenager. When we embrace where we are, we open our hearts to the lessons and blessings of today.

To help you embrace your current season, let's do a simple yet meaningful activity. This activity is a beautiful way to reflect on the current season of parenting while building a habit of gratitude and trust in God.

Materials Needed:

* A jar or small box

* Strips of paper

* A pen

Steps:

Write Down Your Current Season: On a strip of paper, write a few words describing the season of parenting you are in. It could be "toddler chaos," "teen independence," "letting go," or "growing together."

List Blessings and Challenges: Write separate notes for the joys and struggles of this season. Thank God for the joys and surrender the struggles in prayer.

Scripture Encouragement: Write down a Bible verse that brings you peace during this time and place it in the jar.

Revisit Your Jar: Come back to the jar over time and see how God has moved in your journey. Add new prayers and reflections as seasons change.

A PRAYER FOR SEASONS OF IN-BETWEEN

Heavenly Father,

In this season of in-between where the past feels familiar, but the future is uncertain, I come to you seeking peace. Motherhood is a constant change journey filled with moments of joy, challenge, and growth. At times, I feel caught between who I am and who I am becoming, between my child's dependence and their growing independence. In these moments of transition, remind me that you are constant. Lord, help me embrace this season with trust, knowing you guide me and my children. When I feel restless, grant me patience. Fill me with faith when I feel anxious about the future. When I struggle with letting go, reassure me that you are holding my children in your hands. May I find beauty in the waiting, wisdom in the unknown, and gratitude in the present. Let my heart be still in your presence, knowing that no matter what season I find myself in, you are with me, shaping, strengthening, and sustaining me every step of the way.

In Jesus' name, Amen.

MOM GUILT: EMBRACING GRACE OVER PERFECTION

"But he said to me, 'My grace is sufficient for you, for my power is made perfect in weakness.' Therefore I will boast all the more gladly about my weaknesses, so that Christ's power may rest on me."
2 Corinthians 12:9 NIV

Being a parent is one of life's most rewarding yet challenging roles. As mothers, we often carry the weight of expectations, constantly questioning if we are doing enough for our children. While self-reflection is important, it is equally essential to offer ourselves grace. Instead of focusing on every moment, we feel we could have done better, let's shift our perspective to see how God's love and guidance shape our journey in Motherhood.

Mom guilt can creep in when we compare ourselves to unrealistic standards or dwell on mistakes. However, God does not call us perfect mothers; he calls us to be present, loving, and willing to grow. The goal is not to be harsh on yourself but to recognize areas for growth while also celebrating the love, care, and effort you pour into your child each day.

HOW TO OVERCOME MOM GUILT WITH FAITH AND GRACE

* Identify Your Triggers – What situations make you feel inadequate as a mother? Recognizing these patterns can help you address them with prayer and intention.

* Communicate and Ask for Help – You don't have to do it all alone. Lean on God, your loved ones, and your community for support.

* Surround Yourself with Encouragement – Be intentional about spending time with people who uplift and remind you that you are enough.

* Forgive Yourself – Just as God extends grace to us; we must extend it to ourselves. Mistakes are opportunities for growth, not condemnation.

* Release Unrealistic Expectations – Perfection is an impossible standard. Instead, strive for progress, love, and faithfulness in your parenting.

* Shift Your Perspective – Instead of focusing on what you lack, focus on the love you give, the lessons you teach, and the faith you instill in your children.

Activity: Releasing Mom Guilt Through Reflection

Take a moment to journal about a recent experience where you felt your mom's guilt. Ask yourself:

1. What triggered this feeling?

2. Was this guilt based on unrealistic expectations?

3. What truth does God speak over this situation?

4. How can I extend grace to myself moving forward?

End this reflection by asking God to replace your guilt with His peace, reminding yourself that He has chosen you to be your child's mother for a reason.

A PRAYER FOR RELEASING MOM'S GUILT AND EMBRACING GRACE

Heavenly Father,

I come before you with a heart that often feels burdened by guilt, the weight of wondering if I am doing enough, loving enough, or being enough for my children. In my imperfections, I sometimes forget that you never called me to be a perfect mother, only a present one. Lord, remind me that your grace is sufficient, that your power is made perfect in my weakness. Please help me to release the unrealistic expectations I place upon myself and instead embrace the truth that you have chosen me to be my child's mother for a divine purpose. Let me lean into your love instead of my shortcomings, when I fall short. When I make mistakes, remind me that growth comes through grace, not guilt. Lord, fill me with peace in knowing that my worth as a mother is not measured by perfection but by the love, faith, and care I pour into my children daily. Let me trust that you are working in me and through me, shaping not only my child's heart but my own. Thank you for the gift of Motherhood, your unending mercy, and for being my constant source of strength. I surrender my guilt to you and receive your grace with an open heart.

In Jesus' name, Amen.

GOD'S GRACE IN OUR IMPERFECTIONS

"The Lord is compassionate and gracious, slow to anger, abounding in love."
Psalms 103:8 NIV

As we continue embracing grace over perfection, we must remember that our mistakes do not define us; God's love does. We will have moments when we feel like we've fallen short, but instead of carrying guilt, we can choose to carry *grace*.

Mom guilt whispers that we are not doing enough, and should be better patient, and more present. It convinces us that every mistake is a failure. But God gently reminds us that *His grace is greater than our guilt.* He doesn't expect perfection from us, He calls us to rely on Him. He sees every tear, every sacrifice, and every moment of self-doubt, yet He still calls us *worthy.* His grace covers every shortcoming, filling in the gaps where we feel lacking.

God's grace is not just a concept; but an active, unwavering presence in our lives. He does not measure our success by perfection but by our faithfulness. When we bring our struggles before Him, He responds with kindness and understanding, reminding us that *His strength is made perfect in our weakness* (2 Corinthians 12:9).

Instead of dwelling on what we think we lack, let's focus on the *abundance* of love and care we pour into our children daily. Because at the end of the day, it's not about being the perfect mother, it's about being a mother who walks in God's grace, trusting that He is working in us and through us.

Embracing Grace Daily

* Speak Truth Over Yourself – When guilt creeps in, replace it with God's truth: *I am enough because God is enough. His grace covers me.*

* Let Go of Yesterday – Each day is a fresh start. Release past mistakes and focus on the new mercies God gives every morning.

* Celebrate Small Wins – Instead of focusing on what you didn't do, take a moment to acknowledge the moments where you showed love, patience, and faith.

Activity: A Grace Jar

Find a small jar and some slips of paper. Each day, write down how you saw God's grace in your parenting or one way he helped you let go of mom guilt. Pull a note from the jar on difficult days as a reminder that his grace is always present, even when you don't feel it.

A PRAYER FOR EMBRACING GOD'S GRACE IN OUR IMPERFECTIONS

Heavenly Father,

Thank You for your endless grace. When mom guilt weighs me down, remind me that your grace is greater. Please help me to let go of guilt and embrace the truth that I am enough in you. Teach me to see myself through your eyes, loved, chosen, and equipped for this journey of Motherhood. When I fall short, remind me that your grace fills every gap. I surrender my imperfections to you, trusting that you are guiding me every step of the way.

In Jesus' name, Amen.

FAILING FORWARD

"For though the righteous fall seven times, they rise
again, but the wicked stumble when calamity strikes."
Proverbs 24:16 NIV

Motherhood is a journey filled with joy, love, and fulfillment, but it is also a path paved with mistakes, uncertainties, and self-doubt. As mothers, we strive to give our children the best of ourselves. Yet, sometimes when we feel like we have fallen short whether it's losing our patience, making a wrong decision, or struggling to balance our many responsibilities. However, failure in Motherhood is not the end; it is an opportunity to grow, learn, and move forward with grace.

The idea of failing forward means embracing failure as a necessary part of growth rather than a reason for shame or discouragement. It recognizes that each misstep is a lesson, each challenge is a teacher, and each setback is a setup for something greater. God does not expect perfection from us as mothers; He desires progress, faith, and a heart that seeks Him even in our weakest moments. Failure is a powerful teacher. It humbles us, strengthens our character, and deepens our dependence on God. It also teaches our children a valuable lesson: that mistakes are a part of life, and what matters most is how we respond to them.

To fail forward means to keep going, even when things don't go as planned. It means forgiving ourselves, trusting in God's grace, and using our experiences to become wiser, stronger, and more patient. Motherhood is not about getting everything right but about showing up with love, learning as we go, and allowing God to guide our steps. By embracing failure as part of the process, we free ourselves from the pressure of perfection and step into the beauty of God's refining work. **We are not failing; we are growing.** And in that growth, we are becoming exactly who God intended us to be.

A PRAYER FOR FAILING FORWARD

Heavenly Father,

I thank you for the journey of Motherhood, with all its triumphs and challenges. Please help me see failure not as defeat but as an opportunity to grow. When I feel discouraged, please remind me of your grace and the lessons hidden in every mistake. Please give me the strength to keep moving forward, knowing that you are shaping me into the mother you have called me to be.

In Jesus' name, Amen.

Section 2

STRENGTHENING
YOUR FAITH AS A
MOTHER

FAITH OVER FEAR

"So do not fear, for I am with you; do not be dismayed,
for I am your God. I will strengthen you and help you; I
will uphold you with my righteous right hand."
Isaiah 41:10 NIV

If my pride and fear had the final say, I would have never chosen to become a mother at the age of 24. I did not feel equipped or ready for the responsibility that came with this assignment. Doubts flooded my mind: Would I be a good mother? Do I have the wisdom and skills to raise a child? How would Motherhood change my identity? The fear of the unknown loomed over me, threatening to paralyze me before I even began. Yet, regardless of how I felt, I knew that change, growth, and transformation were necessary for me to step fully into the calling God had placed on my life. Motherhood was not just something that happened to me, it was something God used to shape me. He was preparing me for a greater purpose that I could not yet see but was already unfolding before me.

Faith in Motherhood is not always easy. It challenges us to trust God beyond what we can understand. Our faith transforms our circumstances, not because everything suddenly becomes easy, but because we shift our focus from fear to divine purpose. Every phase of Motherhood requires faith, faith to love unconditionally, faith to keep going when exhaustion sets in, and faith to believe that even in our imperfections, God is working all things for good.

One of the greatest struggles I faced was when all three of my children were under three. In that season, I felt my identity had been stripped away. I was no longer just me, I was a mother, completely devoted to the needs of my children. I questioned my purpose and even wondered if God had forgotten about me. But faith reminded me that I was not lost; I was being refined. My identity was not disappearing; it was expanding.

Motherhood is a journey of surrender, where we trust God with the children he entrusted us. It is generational faith that we pass down, one that continue even when uncertainty surrounds us. Hebrews 11:1 says, "Now faith is confidence in what we hope for and assurance about what we do not see" As mothers, we often hope for things we cannot yet see the fruit of our labor, the lessons our children will carry, our prayers' impact on their lives. We walk by faith, knowing that God's promises are true even when not visible. If fear has ever told you that you are not enough, that you will fail, or that your sacrifices are unseen, let me remind you: Every moment of motherhood matters. God sees it all every late night, every whispered prayer, every tear shed in exhaustion, and he is with you. You are not forgotten. You are walking in purpose. You raise the next generation with faith, love, and divine strength.

Today, I chose faith over fear. I trust that God has called me to this journey, and because He has called me, He will equip me. My children are not just my responsibility, they are my ministry. And through every challenge, I know that I am never alone. Revelation 12:2

A Prayer for Faith Over Fear

Heavenly Father,

Thank you for entrusting me with the gift of Motherhood. In moments when fear creeps in, when doubt whispers that I am not enough, remind me that you are my strength. You have called me to this role, and because you have called me, you will equip me. Lord, help me to walk by faith and not by sight. When I feel overwhelmed, anchor me in your promises. When I question my abilities, remind me that my confidence comes not from my strength, but from you. Teach me to surrender my worries, knowing that you guide my steps and hold my children in your loving hands. Father, I lay down my fears at your feet, fear of failure, inadequacy, fear of the unknown and I exchange them for faith. Faith that you have a plan for my children, that you are working in ways I cannot yet see, and that your grace will sustain me through every challenge. Help me to embrace Motherhood not with anxiety, but with the peace that comes from knowing you are always with me. Let my faith be a testimony to my children, a foundation upon which they, too, will learn to trust in you. May my love for them reflect your perfect love for me. I declare today that fear will not rule my heart; faith will. I trust you, Lord, with my motherhood journey, children's future, and growth. Thank you for walking beside me every step of the way.

In Jesus' name, Amen.

SURRENDERING IN MOTHERHOOD

"He gives strength to the weary and increases the power of the weak. Even youths grow tired and weary, and young men stumble and fall; but those who hope in the Lord will renew their strength. They will soar on wings like eagles; they will run and not grow weary; they will walk and not be faint."
Isaiah 40:29-3 NIV

As a mother, surrendering control is one of the hardest lessons. We often feel the weight of responsibility, believing we must do it all; care for our children, manage the household, balance work, and still be emotionally present. But through my own journey, I have realized that after countless moments of burnout, exhaustion, and self-doubt, I cannot do everything alone. I need help. More importantly, I need to trust in God's strength rather than my own.

When I try to rely solely on my strength, I essentially attempt to control the outcome. But the process of surrender of truly releasing my burdens allows God to work in and through me. As mothers, we are often taught that being great means handling everything, even when barely holding on. But letting go does not mean failure, it means accepting reality and recognizing our limitations. It means allowing God to step in where our strength ends.

Psalms 28:7-8 reminds us:
> *"The Lord is my strength and my shield; my heart trusts in Him, and He helps me."*

When we trust in God, He provides a supernatural strength that allows us to release anxiety, worry, and exhaustion. When my children were younger, I worked full-time while trying to manage everything, washing and folding laundry, driving them to extracurricular activities, making dinner, and ensuring their baths and bedtime routines were complete. I constantly felt as though I needed to meet their every need. But the truth is, God never intended us to do it alone. His plans are for us to experience joy and peace in Motherhood, even amidst the trials we face each day. He is always in control.

Here are five ways to practice relinquishing control and surrendering to God's plan in parenting.

1. **Take it one day at a time.** Instead of constantly worrying about the to-do list or striving to meet every demand, focus on being present with your children. Trust that God will equip you for each moment as it comes.

2. **Rely on your support system.** Motherhood was never meant to be a solo journey. Lean on family, friends, and fellow mothers. Build a community that helps carry the load, whether it's through shared responsibilities, prayer, or emotional support.

3. **Embrace change and uncertainty.** Life with children is unpredictable. Plans will shift, challenges will arise, and seasons will change. Instead of resisting, allow yourself to flow with God's plans, knowing He works all things for good.

4. **Let go of perfectionism.** You are not required to be the perfect mother—only a present and loving one. Trust that even your imperfections can be used by God to teach and shape you and your children.

5. **Strengthen your faith through prayer and scripture.** The more time you spend with God, the easier it becomes to surrender control. Cling to His promises and let His Word be your guide in Motherhood.

Here are five bible verses that will help you surrender to the will of God and find freedom in fully trusting him.

Mark
8:34

Romans
12:1

Galations
2:20

Luke
9:3

Jeremiah
12:1

SURRENDERING TO GOD IN PRAYER

Heavenly Father,

Thank you for everything. Thank you for my life, my children, and my family. I am grateful for the gift of salvation you gave me, not by my works, but by your grace. Please teach me to surrender fully to your will and trust your plans for my life. Fill my heart with your love and let me experience the fullness of your presence here on earth. Please show me how to release the pain and trauma of my past and teach me how to forgive as you have forgiven me. Open my eyes and heart to receive the wisdom you want to reveal. Where I feel empty, Lord, fill me with the fruits of the Spirit, love, joy, peace, patience, kindness, goodness, faithfulness, gentleness, and self-control. Continue strengthening my faith and guiding my steps according to your perfect will. Help me parent with love, patience, and grace as I release the need to be in control, trusting that you are always in control.

In Jesus' name, Amen.

PLANTING SEEDS OF FAITH

*"Now faith is confidence in what we hope for and
assurance about what we do not see."*
Hebrews 11:1 NIV

Faith isn't just taught; it's lived. The way we pray, the way we handle challenges, and the way we love others shapes the foundation of our children's relationship with God. Children are naturally observant. They see how we react to hardships, prioritize time with God, and treat others. Our faith becomes a living testimony, showing them what it means to trust God, seek his wisdom, and walk in his love. More than just telling our children about faith, we must model it daily.

WAYS TO LEAD BY EXAMPLE IN FAITH

Prioritize Prayer in Your Home – Let your children see you praying—not just in times of struggle but in gratitude. Encourage them to pray over meals, before bed, and during tough moments.

1. Make Scripture a Part of Everyday Life

Read the Bible together, memorize verses as a family, and discuss what God's Word means daily.

2. Demonstrate Trust in God

When challenges arise, let your children hear you say, ''Let's pray about it, '' instead of reacting with fear or frustration. Show them what it looks like to trust God's plan.

3. Serve Others with a Godly Heart

Whether it's helping a neighbor, volunteering, or simply being kind, teach your children that faith is lived through love and service.

4. Speak Words of Life and Encouragement

Instead of criticism, let your words reflect Christ's love. Speak blessings over your children, affirm their identity in God, and remind them they are deeply loved.

5. Be Honest About Your Faith Journey

It's okay to share your struggles and victories with your children. Let them see faith isn't about perfection but continually seeking God.

Activity: Faith in Action Challenge

As a family, create a "Faith in Action" chart. Write down simple faith-building activities to do together throughout the week, such as:

* Praying for someone in need

* Memorizing a Bible verse

* Writing down three things you're grateful for

* Doing a small act of kindness for a friend or neighbor

At the week's end, reflect together on how these actions strengthened your faith.

A PRAYER FOR GUIDING OUR CHILDREN IN FAITH

Heavenly Father,

Thank you for entrusting me with the gift of raising my children. Help me to lead them in faith, not just with words, but with my actions. Let my life reflect your love, patience, and wisdom. Please give me the strength to be a living example of trust in you. May my children grow to know you deeply and walk boldly in their faith. Let our home be filled with your presence and may everything we do glorify you.

In Jesus' name, Amen.

Reestablishing the spiritual connection with God

"You will seek me and find me when you seek me with
all your heart."
Jeremiah 29:13 NIV

God calls us to renew our minds daily. As followers of Christ, we must recognize that everything is spiritual, including how we think and respond to challenges. When our children misbehave, throw tantrums, or disobey, it can be easy to react in frustration. However, we must remember that they, too, are growing, and their desires of the flesh often lead their actions.

Some may say, "They're just kids," while that may be true, we must also acknowledge that their spirits are constantly receiving. The Holy Spirit is the ultimate teacher, guiding us and our children toward truth. Motherhood is a calling, a holy work, and even in everyday moments, it is an act of worship to God.

Spending intentional time with God allows us to cover our children in prayer, teaching them to walk in the Spirit rather than the flesh. As we model faithfulness, they will grow, their understanding will develop, and their behavior will reflect the transformation. Here are five ways to reestablish the spiritual connection to God with your children

* **Worship with them:** Rejoice and delight yourself in the
  Lord. The atmosphere will change when we worship,

praise, and dance, and God's presence will fill the room.

* **Have bible study with them:** Reading Gods word with your children reminds the enemy that every weapon he tries to form against them cannot prosper.

* **Pray with them:** Rather it's a quick prayer or you are praying over them, proclaiming the word of God over them is a powerful tool knowing that we stand in his armor.

* **Serve them with love:** Think of how patient God is with us and how he gives us unconditional love. Do the same with your kids and pour love into them.

* **Have Family Devotional:** This is a time to be used by God to share his word and testimonies of what he is doing in their lives.

A PRAYER FOR REESTABLISHING THE SPIRITUAL CONNECTION WITH GOD

Heavenly Father,

I come before you with an open heart, longing to draw near to you once again. There have been moments where I have felt distant, distracted by the demands of life and the weight of my responsibilities. Yet, I know that you have never left my side. Your love remains constant, your presence unwavering. Lord, I seek you with all my heart, as your Word promises in Jeremiah

29:13." You will seek me and find me when you seek me with all your heart." I desire to be rooted in your truth; and to walk closely with you in every season of my life. Please help me to silence the noise that pulls me away and to refocus my mind and spirit on you. Renew my faith, refresh my soul, and restore the joy of my salvation. Let my heart hunger for your presence, my mind be filled with your wisdom, and your grace strengthen my spirit. Draw me back into deep fellowship with you so that I may live fully in the peace, purpose, and love you have for me.

In Jesus' name, Amen.

FASTING WITH PURPOSE

"So we fasted and petitioned our God about this, and he
answered our prayer."
Ezra 8:23 NIV

FAST TO INTENSIFY YOUR PRAYERS

* As mothers, we are constantly interceding for our
  children, praying for their protection, wisdom, and
  guidance. Fasting strengthens our prayers, making them
  more focused and intentional as we seek God's covering
  over our children and family.

FAST TO CLARIFY

* Motherhood often brings overwhelming decisions—how
  to discipline, nurture, and guide our children. Fasting
  helps clear the noise and allows us to hear God's voice
  more clearly as we seek wisdom in raising our children.

FAST BECAUSE OF YOUR SIN

* Motherhood can expose our weaknesses—anger,
  impatience, fear, or doubt. Fasting is an opportunity to
  repent, ask for God's grace, and grow into a more Christ-
  like mother, full of love, patience, and understanding.

FAST FOR GOD'S MOVEMENT

* We desire to see God move in our children's lives—
  drawing them closer to him, blessing their futures,
  and fulfilling his promises. Fasting invites his divine
  intervention, shifting our Motherhood from self-reliance
  to full dependence on him.

FAST WHEN FACING PERSECUTION

* Motherhood comes with challenges—judgment from
  others, struggles in parenting, or feeling unappreciated.
  Fasting strengthens us spiritually, reminding us that God
  is our defender, and he equips us to stand firm in our role
  as mothers.

FAST FOR VICTORY DURING TEMPTATION

* The temptation to compare ourselves to other moms,
  to give in to frustration, or to neglect our spiritual well-
  being is real. Fasting helps us overcome these temptations
  and remain steadfast in God's will for our motherhood
  journey.

FAST AS A DISPLAY OF LOVE FOR GOD

* As mothers, our love for God sets the tone for our
  children. When they see us fasting out of devotion and
  love for Him, they learn to prioritize their faith. Our
  example becomes a powerful testimony that shapes their
  spiritual foundation.

Take a moment to reflect on your reasons for fasting. Which of the seven purposes resonates with you the most right now? (Intensifying prayers, seeking clarity, repentance, seeking God's movement, facing persecution, overcoming temptation, or displaying love for God).

* Write about what you are fasting for and how you hope it will impact your life as a mother.

* What emotions or struggles do you anticipate during this fast? How will you rely on God's strength to overcome them?

* Reflect on a scripture that encourages you during fasting (e.g., Matthew 6:16-18 or Isaiah 58:6-9). How does this scripture speak to your heart?

A PRAYER FOR FASTING WITH PURPOSE

Heavenly Father,

I come before you with a heart longing to draw closer to you. As I enter this time of fasting, I surrender my desires, struggles and burdens to you, knowing that you are my source of strength and wisdom. Your Word in Ezra 8:23 reminds me that when we fast and seek you wholeheartedly, you hear and answer our prayers. Lord, I fast with purpose, trusting that you will move mightily in my life and my children lives. Help me to intercede for my children with greater intensity, covering them in prayer and entrusting them to your divine protection and guidance. When I face uncertainty in my motherhood journey, grant me clarity and wisdom to nurture them in your ways. Where I have fallen short, let this fast be a time of repentance, renewal, and transformation, shaping me into a mother who reflects your love and patience. Father, I ask for your movement in my home, my children's hearts and every aspect of our lives. Strengthen me when I feel weary, uplift me when I face persecution or doubt, and guard my heart against comparison and discouragement.

May this fast be an act of love and devotion to you, a testimony of faith that my children will witness and one day follow. Sustain me through this journey, Lord. When hunger or weakness sets in, let it remind me of my deep need for you. When struggles arise, help me to lean on your grace. May this fast bring breakthrough, renewal, and deeper intimacy with you.

In Jesus' name, Amen.

THE IMPORTANCE OF REST

"Come to me, all you who are weary and burdened, and I will give you rest. Take my yoke upon you and learn from me, for I am gentle and humble in heart, and you will find rest for your souls. For my yoke is easy and my burden is light."
Matthew 11:28-30 NIV

Society glorifies busyness, making many mothers feel guilty for resting, but God calls us to embrace his gift of rest. Rest is not a luxury; it's a necessity. Even Jesus, during his ministry, took moments to withdraw and be refreshed (Luke 5:16). If the Son of God needed rest, how much more do we? True rest is not just about sleep; it's about surrender. It's trusting that God is in control, even when we pause from our to-do lists.

WHY REST MATTERS IN MOTHERHOOD:

1. Rest Strengthens Us for the Journey – Physical and spiritual exhaustion leads to burnout. When we rest, we allow God to renew our energy for the work he entrusted us.

2. Rest Teaches Dependence on God – Taking time to step back reminds us that we are not the source of everything—God is.

3. Rest Sets an Example for Our Children – When our children see us prioritizing peace and balance, they also learn to value rest and self-care.

4. Rest is an Act of Worship – Sabbath rest allows us to realign with God, refocus on his voice, and restore our souls.

PRACTICAL WAYS TO EMBRACE REST AS A MOM:

* Start your day with prayer, even if it's moments of stillness before the chaos begins.

* Take breaks when needed without guilt—your worth is not in your productivity.

* Create a Sabbath routine where you slow down and spend intentional time with God and loved ones.

* Set boundaries—say no to unnecessary stress and yes to things that nourish your soul.

* Let go of perfection—your home, parenting and schedule don't have to be flawless. Trust God in the mess.

Activity: Creating a Rest Plan

1. Take a moment to reflect on your daily routine and ask yourself:

2. What are the biggest drains on my energy?

3. How can I intentionally incorporate small moments of rest throughout my day?

4. What is one way I can invite God's presence into my rest?

5. How can I model healthy rest for my children?

Write down one commitment you'll make to prioritize rest this week. Whether it's setting aside quiet time with God, getting enough sleep, or simply permitting yourself to pause, remember that rest is not selfish, it's sacred.

A Prayer for Resting in Faith

Heavenly Father,

Thank you for the gift of rest. Please help me to release the pressure of always doing and embrace the peace that comes from being still with you. Remind me that I am enough, even when I pause. Teach me to trust you with my responsibilities so I can find true rest in your presence.

In Jesus' name, Amen.

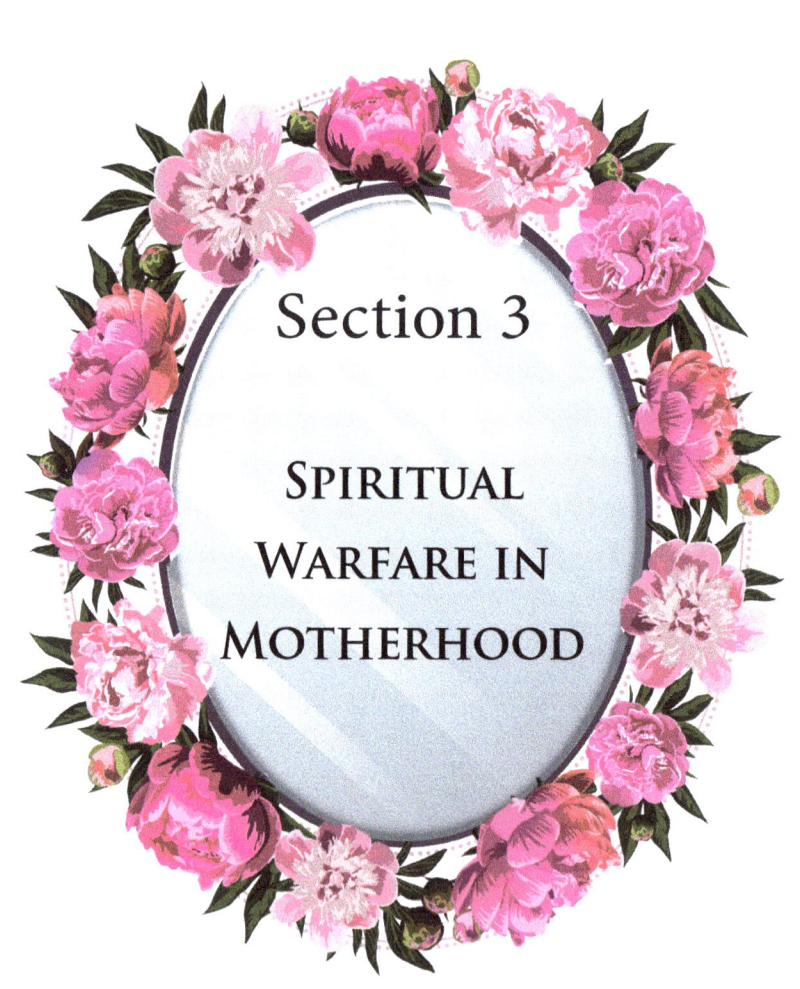

Section 3

SPIRITUAL
WARFARE IN
MOTHERHOOD

Spiritual Warfare in Motherhood

"The thief comes only to steal and kill and destroy; I have come that they may have life, and have it to the full."
John 10:10 NIV

Motherhood is a spiritual calling, but it is also a battlefield. Satan's tactics to steal, kill, and destroy (John 10:10) are evident in the daily struggles we face as mothers. He seeks to attack our peace, distort our identity, and create division between us and our children. We may find ourselves choosing anger over love, frustration over patience, and fear over faith. These choices, often made in moments of exhaustion, can become habits that hinder our ability to reflect Christ in our homes. However, God has equipped us with spiritual armor (Ephesians 6:10-18) to stand firm against these attacks.

When Satan Attacks

God's revelation comes **FIRST**; the enemy comes **SECOND** to steal the revelation. Satan will also try to quicken the vision. Satan will attempt to confuse you with the instructions God gives you. The devil is loud to get you to prove yourself. Now that I am aware of when Satan attacks, I am ready to fight the enemy to prevail over his tactics.

Taking Authority in Spiritual Warfare

Now that I am aware of the enemy's strategies, I choose to:

* Replace doubt with faith

* Replace anger with love

* Replace fear with trust in God

* Replace chaos with God's peace

A Prayer for Strength

Heavenly Father,

I recognize that I am engaged in spiritual warfare as a mother. The enemy seeks to steal my peace, joy, and confidence in you. But I declare that I am covered by your grace and equipped with your word. I reject fear, anxiety, and frustration, and I choose to stand firm in your truth. Strengthen me to lead my children in love and to overcome the tactics of the enemy.

In Jesus' name, Amen.

How Satan Targets Motherhood

*"Put on the full armor of God, so that you can take your
stand against the devil's schemes."*
Ephesians 6:11 NIV

1. Satan repeatedly brings suffering into our lives, attempting to weaken our ability to love and serve our children with a Christ-centered heart.

2. Satan twists the truth, making us doubt God's promises and rely on our strength instead of His guidance

3. Satan attacks our minds to make us feel inadequate and incapable of being a mother.

4. Satan uses comparison to make us feel like we are not good enough.

5. Satan uses the SAME tactics because he knows our triggers

A Prayer for Protection in Motherhood

Heavenly Father,

I come before you today, seeking your divine protection and strength in my journey as a mother. I know that the enemy seeks to attack, discourage, and distract me from the calling you have placed on my life. He tries to plant seeds of fear, doubt, and guilt, making me question my worth and ability to raise my children in your truth. But, Lord, I reject his lies and stand firm in your promises today. Cover me with your full armor, O God. Strengthen my heart with your truth, shield my mind from deception, and guard my family against the enemy's schemes. When exhaustion creeps in, remind me that you are my rest. When doubt whispers, reassure me of my purpose. When fear takes hold, fill me with unwavering faith. I lift my children to you, Lord, knowing they belong to you first. Protect their hearts, guide their steps, and draw them closer to you each day. Give me wisdom to lead them well, patience to nurture them with grace, and faith to trust you in every season. Thank you, Father, for equipping me for this calling. I will not be shaken, for you go before me. The enemy has no place in my home, no power over my mind, and no hold on my family. I walk in victory, for I am a mother chosen and anointed by you.

In Jesus' name, Amen.

Spiritual Battle Between Flesh and Spirit

"So I say, walk by the Spirit, and you will not gratify the desires of the flesh. For the flesh desires what is contrary to the Spirit, and the Spirit what is contrary to the flesh. They are in conflict with each other, so that you are not to do whatever you want."

Galatians 5:16-17 NIV

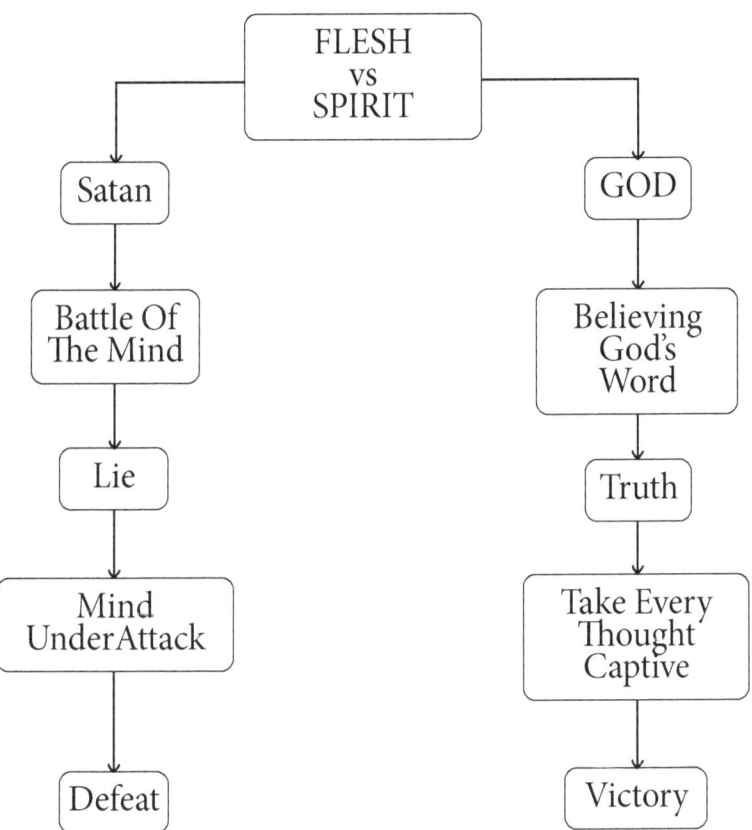

PRAYER FOR OVERCOMING THE BATTLE OF THE MIND

Heavenly Father,

I come before you today, surrendering my mind and thoughts into your hands. The battle between flesh and spirit is real, and the enemy seeks to plant lies in my heart. But I declare that your truth is greater! Lord, help me to take every thought captive and make it obedient to Christ (2 Corinthians 10:5). When my mind is under attack, remind me of your promises, that I am fearfully and wonderfully made (Psalms 139:14), that I am more than a conqueror through Christ (Romans 8:37), and that I have the mind of Christ (1 Corinthians 2:16). When the enemy whispers lies of fear, doubt, and defeat, strengthen me to stand firm in your Word. Fill me with your peace, reminding me that you have not given me a spirit of fear but of power, love, and a sound mind (2 Timothy 1:7). I rebuke every lie and deception that tries to take root in my spirit. Instead, I choose to walk in victory, knowing that you are with me, fighting on my behalf. Thank you for renewing my mind daily and leading me toward truth.

In Jesus' name, Amen.

Becoming Unshakable

"No weapon forged against you will prevail, and you will refute every tongue that accuses you."
Isaiah 54:17 NIV

We are warriors, armed with the power of God, and through Him, we will not be shaken. To become unshakable means to rise above the enemy's attacks and stand firm in our identity as mothers called and chosen by God. It means silencing the lies with the truth of God's Word, rejecting fear with faith, and fighting for our families in the spirit. When we walk in the authority Christ has given us, no attack of the enemy can stand.

Claiming Victory Over Spiritual Warfare

1. Recognize the Battle and Fight with Prayer

The enemy attacks through worry, discouragement, and fear. Instead of reacting to stress, respond in prayer. Cover your children, your home, and your mind in God's protection daily.

2. Declare God's Authority Over Your Home–

Speak life over your children, your marriage, and your household. Rebuke fear and anxiety in Jesus' name, and proclaim that no weapon formed against you will prosper. (Isaiah 54:17)

3. Use Worship as a Weapon

When you feel overwhelmed, worship shifts the atmosphere. Praise God in the midst of the storm, and watch how fear and doubt lose their grip.

4. Stand on God's Promises, Not Your Feelings

Feelings change, but God's truth remains. When the enemy tries to shake you, anchor yourself in His Word. You are equipped, chosen, and empowered to raise your children in faith.

5. Refuse to Let Fear Dictate Your Motherhood

Fear has no authority over a woman covered by the blood of Jesus. When worry creeps in, reject it with faith. Trust that God is in control, and His plans for your children are greater than any enemy attack.

Activity: Declaring Your Victory in Christ

Write down three lies the enemy has tried to make you believe about yourself as a mother. Then, find and write down three scriptures that declare God's truth over those lies. Speak these truths daily until they become your reality.

For example:

* **Lie**: *I am not a good enough mother.*
  Truth: *"God is within her; she will not fall; God will help her at break of day."* — Psalms 46:5

* **Lie**: *I am failing my children.*
  Truth: *"The Lord is faithful, and He will strengthen you and protect you from the evil one."* — 2 Thessalonians 3:3

* **Lie**: *I am too weak to do this.*
Truth: *"But the Lord is faithful; He will establish you and guard you against the evil one."* — 2 Thessalonians 3:3

You are not just a mother; and you are a warrior. Walk boldly in the power God has given you. The battle has already been won.

A Prayer for Becoming Unshakable

Heavenly Father,

I come before you, seeking the strength that only you can provide. In the midst of Motherhood's challenges, uncertainties, and spiritual battles, I desire to stand firm, unshakable in my faith, unwavering in my trust, and unmovable in my purpose. Lord, the storms of life may come, but I know that when I am rooted in you, I will not be shaken. Strengthen me to resist fear, doubt, and discouragement. When I feel weary, be my rest. When I feel overwhelmed, be my peace. When I feel uncertain, be my confidence. Let your truth be my foundation, wisdom, guide, and your love be my covering. Please help me Lord, lead my children by example; to show them what it means to trust you wholeheartedly. Let them see a mother who stands on your promises, prays with boldness, and loves with the strength that only comes from you. I declare that I am unshakable because I am anchored in Christ. No weapon formed against me will prosper, no fear will consume me, and no trial will break me. I hope in you and I will stand firm through you.

In Jesus' mighty name, Amen.

Section 4

THE POWER OF
PRAYER & BIBLICAL
ENCOURAGEMENT

The Power of Prayer Over Our Children

"The prayer of a righteous person is powerful and effective."
James 5:16 NIV

As mothers, we have the incredible privilege and responsibility of praying for our children. In a world of uncertainties, our greatest defense is not in our own strength but in surrendering our children to God's hands through prayer. Prayer is not just a routine or a last resort; it is a powerful covering, a shield that surrounds our children with God's presence. We invite his protection, wisdom, and grace into their lives through prayer. The enemy seeks to steal, kill, and destroy (John 10:10), but God is our refuge and fortress (Psalms 91:2). When we pray, we align ourselves with His will and declare His promises over our children.

Praying for Protection

Psalms 91:11 reminds us, "For He will command His angels concerning you to guard you in all your ways." As mothers, we can trust that God's angels are watching over our children. Whether they are at home, at school, or venturing into new seasons of life, we can pray that His divine protection surrounds them.

Praying for Their Hearts and Minds

In a world that constantly seeks to shape our children's identities, we must pray for their hearts and minds to be anchored in God's truth.

Philippians 4:7 says, "And the peace of God, which transcends all understanding, will guard your hearts and minds in Christ Jesus." May our prayers fill their hearts with peace, courage, and wisdom.

PRAYING FOR THEIR FUTURE

God has a divine purpose for each child. Jeremiah 29:11 declares, "For I know the plans I have for you, declares the Lord, plans to prosper you and not to harm you, plans to give you hope and a future." We can pray that our children walk in God's plans, making choices that honor Him and lead them into a life of purpose and joy.

Activity: A Prayer Covering for Your Child

STEP 1: CREATE A PRAYER JOURNAL FOR YOUR CHILD

Dedicate a notebook to writing prayers for your child.

Write about their protection, spiritual growth, friendships, and future.

Include Bible verses that align with your prayers.

STEP 2: DAILY PRAYER OF COVERING

Each morning or evening, pray these words over your child:

"Heavenly Father, I thank You for the precious gift of my child. I ask for Your protection over them, guard their heart, mind, and body from harm. Cover them with Your peace and wisdom and let them walk in Your ways. Surround them with godly influences and let them always hear Your voice above the world's noise. I entrust them into

Your loving hands. In Jesus' name, Amen."

STEP 3: BLESSING YOUR CHILD

Speak words of encouragement over them.

If possible, lay hands on them and pray with them.

Let them hear you declare God's promises over their life.

REFLECTION QUESTIONS:

1. How can I be more intentional about praying for my child daily?

2. In what ways have I seen God's protection in my child's life?

3. What Bible verses can I use to pray specifically over my child?

A MOTHER'S PRAYER

"The prayer of a righteous person is powerful and
effective."
James 5:16 NIV

Heavenly Father,

Thank you for the precious gift of my child. I lift
them to you today, knowing you love them even
more than I do. You have created them purpose-
fully, and I trust in your perfect plan for their lives.

Lord, I ask for your divine protection over them. Guard
their heart, mind, and body from harm. Surround them
with your angels, shielding them from danger, temptation, and anything that would seek to pull them away
from you. Let no weapon be formed against them prosper and let them always dwell in the shelter of your love.

I pray for their heart and mind, to be filled with your wisdom,
peace, and truth. In a world that tries to define them, may they
always find their identity in you. Let their thoughts be fixed
on what is good, pure, and righteous. Strengthen their faith
so they may stand firm against the pressures of this world.

Lord, I surrender their future into your hands. I trust that you are
leading them on the right path, guiding their steps, and open-
ing doors that align with your will. May they always seek you
in every decision, knowing that your plans for them are good.

Lord, help me be a mother who prays with intention and faith. Let my words be filled with encouragement, my actions reflect your love, and my heart be steadfast in lifting them before you daily.

I declare that my child is covered by your grace, protected by your love, and led by your Spirit.

In Jesus' name, Amen.

BIBLICAL AFFIRMATIONS FOR MOTHERHOOD

*"The tongue has the power of life and death, and those
who love it will eat its fruit".*
Proverbs 18:21 NIV

Biblical affirmations play a powerful role in overcoming negative feelings, thoughts, and situations. As you declare these affirmations, ask God to help you see yourself through his eyes and grant you a renewed perspective on your journey as a mother. Stand firm in God's truth when the enemy attacks your mind with doubt or discouragement. Remember his power to take every thought captive and align your heart with his Word.

* I am fearfully and wonderfully made (Psalms 139:14)

* No weapon formed against me will prosper (Isaiah 54:17)

* I am anointed by God (1 John 2:27)

* I have an abundance for every good work (2 Corinthians 9:8)

* My family is blessed, my flocks are blessed (Deuteronomy 28:4)

* I am the head and not the tail (Deuteronomy 28:13)

* I can do all things through Christ who strengthens me (Philippians 4:13)

* I lack no good thing (Psalms 34:1)

* I was predestined by God for success (Romans 8:28)

* God will never leave me nor forsake me (Hebrews 13:5)

THE SEVEN CHARACTERISTICS OF THE HOLY SPIRIT

1. Comforter – John 14:16

"And I will ask the Father, and he will give you another Comforter to help you and be with you forever."

2. Counselor – Isaiah 11:2

"The Spirit of the Lord will rest on him—the Spirit of wisdom and understanding, the Spirit of counsel and might, the Spirit of knowledge and fear of the Lord."

3. Helper – Psalms 121:1-2

"I lift up my eyes to the mountains—where does my help come from? My help comes from the Lord, the Maker of heaven and earth."

4. Intercessor – Romans 8:26

"In the same way, the Spirit helps us in our weakness. We do not know what we ought to pray for, but the Spirit himself intercedes for us through wordless groans."

5. Advocate – John 14:26

"But the Advocate, the Holy Spirit, whom the Father will send in my name, will teach you everything and remind you of everything I have said to you."

6. Strengthener – Ephesians 3:16

"I pray that out of his glorious riches he may strengthen you with power through his Spirit in your inner being."

7. Protector – 2 Thessalonians 3:3

"But the Lord is faithful, and he will strengthen you and protect you from the evil one."

Take a moment to reflect on each of the seven characteristics of the Holy Spirit: Comforter, Counselor, Helper, Intercessor, Advocate, Strengthener, and Protector.

1. Which of these characteristics have you experienced most in your motherhood journey?

2. What area of your life do you need the Holy Spirit's guidance and presence the most?

Activity: Holy Spirit Reflection Cards

Create seven index cards or journal entries, each dedicated to one of the characteristics of the Holy Spirit.

On each card, write:

* The characteristic (e.g., Comforter)

* A scripture that relates to it (e.g., John 14:16 - "And I will ask the Father, and he will give you another Comforter to help you and be with you forever.")

* A personal reflection or example of how you have seen this characteristic.

Each day, choose one card and meditate on that aspect of the Holy Spirit. Journal your thoughts, prayers, and any insights you receive.

A PRAYER FOR GUIDANCE

Heavenly Father,

I come before you in gratitude for the gift of the Holy Spirit, who is ever-present in my life. Lord, I invite your Spirit to fill my heart and guide my Motherhood journey. When I feel weary, be my **Comforter**, wrapping me in your peace and reminding me that I am never alone (John 14:16). When I am uncertain, be my **Counselor**, granting me wisdom and discernment in every decision I make (Isaiah 11:2). Lord, when I feel overwhelmed, be my **Helper**, lifting my burdens and strengthening me with your grace (Psalms 121:1-2). When I struggle to find the words to pray, be my **Intercessor**, speaking on my behalf with groanings too deep for words (Romans 8:26). Holy Spirit, be my **Advocate**, teaching me, reminding me of God's promises, and reassuring me that I am equipped for this calling (John 14:26). In moments of exhaustion and doubt, be my **Strengthener**, renewing my spirit and filling me with divine power (Ephesians 3:16). And, Lord, in the face of trials and challenges, be my **Protector**, shielding me and my children from harm and leading us in your truth (2 Thessalonians 3:3). I surrender every aspect of my Motherhood to you. May your Spirit fill my home with love, peace, and faith. Let Your presence be my constant guide, and may I reflect your goodness in all I do.

In Jesus' name, Amen.

Section 5

HEALING,
GROWTH, AND
COMMUNITY IN
MOTHERHOOD

Grieving the Old You

*"Forget the former things; do not dwell on the past. See,
I am doing a new thing! Now it springs up; do you not
perceive it? I am making a way in the wilderness and
streams in the wasteland."*
Isaiah 43:18-19 NIV

Embracing the New Season of Motherhood

Motherhood is a beautiful transformation, but with it often comes a silent grief, one that many mothers struggle to name. I found myself mourning my old life, the life I had before my children. After giving birth, I felt an overwhelming sense of loss, a loss of normalcy, a loss of intimacy, and even a loss of emotional stability. While it was one of the most life-altering and sacred moments, it also brought unexpected challenges.

Early on, it wasn't easy to stay present. My mind constantly raced between responsibilities, to-do lists, and the ever-growing weight of Motherhood. I longed for the freedom I once had, the ability to rest without interruption; and enjoy simple moments without exhaustion. I grieved my old life and looked forward to the quiet moments when my children were asleep, when I could finally breathe.

Much of this grief stemmed from unrealistic expectations, ideals shaped by a world that tells us Motherhood should look a certain way. Society often romanticizes Motherhood, making it seem like a season of pure joy and fulfillment. But the truth is, the transition into

Motherhood is complex. There is beauty, but there is also sacrifice. And sometimes, what we feel contradicts what God says.

In Matthew 26:38, even Jesus experienced deep sorrow: "My soul is overwhelmed with sorrow to the point of death." He grieved, knowing the suffering he would endure. Yet, despite his agony, he surrendered to God's will, trusting that something greater was on the other side of his pain. This reminds us that grief is not a sign of weakness, but a natural part of transformation. And just as God comforted Jesus, he comforts us in our sorrow, especially in the losses we experience as we step into Motherhood.

Yet, God does not leave us in grief. He calls us to move forward, to step into the new identity he has given us. Proverbs 4:25-27 encourages us: "Let your eyes look straight ahead; fix your gaze directly before you. Give careful thought to the paths for your feet and be steadfast in all your ways." God reassures us that looking back is not the answer. Instead, he invites us to embrace what he is birthing in this new season.

Reflection Activity: Honoring Your Past, Embracing Your Future

Take a moment to reflect on the parts of your old life you miss. Write them down in a journal. Then, beside each one, write how Motherhood has brought a new blessing into your life. This is not to dismiss your grief but to help you see that God is using this transition to shape you into something even greater.

Ask yourself:

1. What aspects of my old life do I grieve the most?

2. How has Motherhood changed me for the better?

3. How can I surrender my grief to God and trust His plan for this season?

As you reflect, remember: God is not asking you to forget who you were before Motherhood. Instead, he guides you into the fullness of who you are becoming.

A Prayer for Grieving the Old You

Heavenly Father,

In this season of change, I bring my grief to you. I mourn the parts of me that feel lost, yet I trust that you are doing a new thing within me. Please help me to release what was and embrace what is, knowing that you are shaping me for a greater purpose. Fill my heart with peace and remind me that my identity is secure in you. Thank you for walking with me through this transformation.

In Jesus' name, Amen.

FORGIVENESS

*"Be kind and compassionate to one another, forgiving
each other, just as in Christ God forgave you."*
Ephesians 4:32 NIV

Cultivating forgiveness creates more space for love, growth, and a
deeper connection between a mother and child. As parents, we often
expect how our children should behave, it can be difficult to respond
with grace when they act in ways that challenge what we have taught
them. However, true forgiveness is not about excusing mistakes but
rather about choosing love over resentment.

Oftentimes, we undermine forgiveness because of the unrealistic
expectations we place on ourselves and others. This can lead to frustration, distance, and even a strained relationship with our children.
But just as God extends endless mercy to us, we are called to do the
same, for our children and ourselves. Forgiveness is a continual process
that fosters healing, peace, and emotional freedom within the family.

Reflection Activity: The Forgiveness Box

Take a moment to reflect on any situations where forgiveness is needed
in your home, whether forgiving your child for disobedience, yourself
for moments of frustration or others who may have influenced your
parenting journey.

1. Create a Forgiveness Box – Choose a small box and write your
   child's name. If you have multiple children, create a box for each
   one.

2. Write it Down – On small pieces of paper, write an apology note, a frustration you need to release, or a prayer for guidance in extending grace. Place each note inside the box.

3. Pray Over the Box – Ask God to remove any spirit of unforgiveness, bitterness, or guilt lingering in your heart. Pray that your relationship with your child remains rooted in love, patience, and understanding.

Remember, forgiveness does not mean forgetting, but choosing to move forward with peace in your heart. Just as God's mercies are new every morning (Lamentations 3:22-23), may we extend fresh grace to ourselves and our children daily.

PRAYER FOR FORGIVENESS

Heavenly Father,

Thank you for the gift of forgiveness. Just as you have forgiven me time and time again, help me to extend that same grace to my children. When frustration arises, remind me of your perfect love. Soften my heart, Lord, so I may forgive quickly and love uncon-ditionally. I surrender any bitterness, anger, or resentment linger-ing, and I ask for your peace to fill my home. Teach me to model your grace; so that my child may learn the beauty of forgiveness.

In Jesus' name, Amen.

THE POWER OF UNITY IN MOTHERHOOD

"And over all these virtues put on love, which binds them all together in perfect unity"
Colossians 3:14 NIV

Unity is a cornerstone of Motherhood, fostering a sense of togetherness, support, and understanding within our families and communities. Regardless of cultural backgrounds or personal experiences, the bond between a mother and her child, and the relationships we cultivate with others are strengthened when we prioritize unity. When we embrace unity, we create a foundation of love, respect, and cooperation that nurtures our children and ourselves as mothers.

Prioritizing unity means being intentional about fostering deep and meaningful connections. It requires patience, empathy, and a willingness to meet each child where they are emotionally, mentally, and spiritually. Motherhood is not a solitary journey, but a shared experience that thrives on connection and mutual growth.

Reflection Activity: Strengthening Your Bond

I challenge you to take time with each of your children individually. Set aside dedicated moments to truly listen, observe, and understand them on a deeper level. Each child has unique needs, love languages, and ways of expressing themselves. Focusing on them individually creates a safe space where they feel seen, heard, and valued.

Here are a few ways to cultivate unity in your home:

* One-on-One Time – Plan special outings or quiet moments at home with each child to foster deeper conversations and connections.

* Prayer and Reflection – Pray together and invite your child to share their thoughts, worries, and joys.

* Encourage Teamwork – Create family activities that require collaboration, emphasizing that each member plays a valuable role.

* Model Unity – Demonstrate patience, kindness, and grace in daily interactions, showing your children the beauty of working together in love.

Unity strengthens our families and glorifies God, reflecting His design for relationships. As Psalms 133:1 says, *"How good and pleasant it is when God's people live together in unity!"* Let this remind you to nurture unity in your home to flourish love and connection.

A Prayer for Unity

Heavenly Father,

Thank you for the gift of Motherhood and the bond that unites us with our children and fellow mothers. Help us to foster love, patience, and understanding in our homes, creating a foundation of unity that reflects your heart. Teach us to listen with compassion, nurture with grace, and lead with wisdom. May our families be a testament to the beauty of together-ness and may our love for one another glorify you. Bind us in perfect unity, Lord, and let our homes be filled with peace.

In Jesus' name, Amen.

FILL UP YOUR CUP!

*"May the God of hope fill you with all joy and peace as
you trust in him, so that you may overflow with hope by
the power of the Holy Spirit."*
Romans 15:13 NIV

As mothers, we are natural givers, pouring our time, energy, and love
into our families. But how can we continue to pour it into others when
our cup is empty? Jesus invites us to rest in Him, to replenish our
spirit, and to embrace self-care as an act of faith. When prioritizing our
well-being, we become better mothers, partners, and women of God.

Take a moment to reflect:

* What does self-care look like to you?

* How do you currently prioritize your emotional, spiritual,
  and physical well-being?

* In what ways can you invite God into your self-care
  routine?

Activity: Create Your Ideal Self-Care Day. Imagine a full day
dedicated to refilling your cup. Write down activities that bring you
peace, joy, and renewal. Your list might include:

* A slow morning with coffee and quiet prayer

* Reading scripture or a devotional

* Taking a relaxing bath

* A walk in nature, listening to worship music

* Journaling your thoughts and prayers

* Engaging in a hobby or pampering yourself

Now, choose **one thing you can do this week** to nurture yourself. Schedule it, commit to it, and embrace it to honor the temple God has given you.

A PRAYER FOR OVERFLOW

Heavenly Father,

I come before you weary and in need of renewal. Pour your peace into my heart, your strength into my spirit, and your love into my soul. In the busyness of Motherhood, please remind me to pause and rest in your presence. Fill my cup, Lord, to pour love, patience, and kindness into those around me. Let your grace sustain me, and your joy refresh me. May I never give from emptiness but always from the abundance of your overflowing goodness.

In Jesus' name, Amen.

Embracing Your Inner Child Through God's Love

"Let the little children come to me, and do not hinder
them, for the kingdom of God belongs to such as these."
Matthew 19:14 NIV

As a mother, your love and guidance shape your children's lives, but you must also nurture the little girl within you to nurture them fully. Your inner child is the part of you that once longed for safety, belonging, and unconditional love. The good news is that God has always seen her, cherished her, and held her close. Take a moment to reflect: What were the deepest needs of your childhood heart? What words of comfort, encouragement, and reassurance would have brought you peace? Now, imagine God whispering those words to you. His love is boundless, healing the wounds of the past and filling you with strength for the present.

You are not alone in this journey of self-acceptance and healing. As you embrace your past with grace, you create a foundation of love and security, for yourself and your children. When you allow God to heal your inner child, you are better equipped to guide your little ones with wisdom, patience, and a heart overflowing with His love.

Write a heartfelt letter to yourself, one filled with grace, forgiveness, and understanding. Speak to the little girl within you as God speaks to His beloved daughter. Remind her that she is safe, valued, and deeply loved, both by you and by her Heavenly Father. Then write a heartfelt letter to your children as a reminder that they are unconditionally loved, not just by you, but by God, who created them with purpose and intention. Your words will stand as a beacon of truth, reminding them that they are enough just as they are. It reassures them that they will never walk alone, and that no mistake or hardship can separate them from your love or God's grace.

A LETTER TO YOURSELF

A Letter to Your Children

Section 6

RAISING GODLY
CHILDREN

Train Up a Child

"Start children off on the way they should go, and even when they are old they will not turn from it"
Proverbs 22:6 NIV

Many parents experience shame, guilt, or self-doubt when their children do not follow the path they had envisioned. As a mother, it is easy to question yourself—*Did I do enough? Was I too strict? Too :lenient?*—especially when your children struggle, rebel, or take a path contrary to what you had hoped. However, God's Word offers us guidance and reassurance.

Proverbs 22:6 states, *"Train up a child in the way he should go, and when he is old, he will not depart from it."* This verse serves as both an instruction and a promise. Our role as parents is to lay the foundation, instilling faith, morals, and values during their formative years. Once they grow and begin making their own choices, it is ultimately between them and God to continue that path or to stray. But the seeds we plant will always remain within them.

Meditating on this scripture, I realized that our role as parents is not about controlling the outcome but faithfully stewarding the process. We are called to *train*, nurture, guide, and equip our children with God's truth. Whether they follow it immediately or take a longer journey back to it, our obedience in raising them in faith is not in vain.

God's Purpose for Our Children

Think of it this way: God has a divine purpose for us. From the moment Jesus entered the world, His purpose was clear, to save humanity from sin. Likewise, every child born into this world has a unique calling from God, even though they enter with a natural inclination toward sin. As parents, we are responsible for training them in righteousness, guiding them toward their God-given purpose, and trusting that God is working in their lives even when we cannot see it.

Our children will learn from the world around them, whether we teach them or not. This is why it is crucial that we must take the time to instill the *foundation* of God's Word in them. We are not merely raising children; we are raising future men and women of faith who will carry the light of Christ into the world. The seeds we plant today will bear fruit in due time, even if there are seasons of struggle along the way.

LETTING GO AND TRUSTING GOD

One of the hardest lessons in Motherhood is learning to let go and trust that God is in control. We may wish to protect our children from every hardship, but ultimately, they must walk their faith journey. Our role is to equip them, pray over them, and continue to demonstrate unwavering faith in our own lives. Isaiah 64:8 reminds us, *"Yet you, Lord, are our Father. We are the clay, you are the potter; we are all the work of your hand."* Just as God molds and shapes us through our experiences, He is doing the same for our children.

Even when we struggle as mothers, when we feel inadequate or unsure, God is also using our parenting journey to refine us. Raising children is not just about shaping them but also about allowing God to shape *us* into stronger, more faithful followers of Christ. Every challenge in Motherhood is an opportunity to grow in grace, patience, and trust.

ENCOURAGEMENT FOR MOTHERS

If you have ever felt like you failed in raising your children, be encouraged: God sees your efforts, and He is faithful to complete the work He has started in both you and your children (Philippians 1:6). Keep praying, keep trusting, and keep planting seeds of faith. No act of love, lesson taught, or prayer whispered over your children is ever wasted.

Reflection Questions:

In what ways are you intentionally training your children in faith?

How can you surrender your worries about your children's future to God?

What prayers can you begin praying over your children today?

SCRIPTURE FOR MEDITATION:

* **Proverbs 22:6** – *"Train up a child in the way he should go, and when he is old, he will not depart from it."*

* **Isaiah 64:8** – *"Yet you, Lord, are our Father. We are the clay, you are the potter; we are all the work of your hand."*

* **Philippians 1:6** – *"Being confident of this, that he who began a good work in you will carry it on to completion until the day of Christ Jesus."*

A PRAYER FOR TRAINING UP A CHILD

Heavenly Father,

Thank you for the gift of my children and the privilege of raising them in your love and truth. I ask for wisdom, patience, and discernment as I guide them on the path you have set before them. Help me to train them up in faith, to plant seeds of righteousness, and to model a life that reflects your grace and goodness. When I feel weary or uncertain, remind me that my efforts are not in vain. Strengthen my heart to trust in your promises, knowing that the foundation I build today will bear fruit in your perfect time. Even when my children face struggles or stray, let me rest in the assurance that you are always at work in their hearts. Lord, I release my fears and anxieties about their future into your hands. You are the Potter, they are the clay; mold them according to your divine purpose. Cover them with your protection, fill them with your wisdom, and draw them closer to you each day. May they grow to love you deeply, walk in your ways, and fulfill the calling you have placed on their lives. I entrust them to you, Lord, knowing your love for them is even greater than mine.

In Jesus' name, Amen.

Speaking Life – The Power of Words

*"But I tell you that everyone will have to give account
on the day of judgment for every empty word they have
spoken. For by your words you will be acquitted, and by
your words you will be condemned."*
Matthew 12:36-37 NIV

As mothers, our words shape the hearts and minds of our children.
Every word we speak has the power to build them up or tear them
down. Scripture reminds us that our tongues hold the power of life
and death, and as we guide our children in faith, it is essential to teach
them how to use their words to uplift, encourage, and glorify God.

In the fast-paced journey of Motherhood, it can be easy to let frustration spill into our words, but God calls us to speak life. Our children
look to us as examples, and when we model grace, kindness, and
faith-filled speech, they learn to do the same. Teaching them to guard
their tongues, speak truth in love, and encourage others reflects the
heart of Christ.

We affirm their worth in Christ when we speak life over our children.
Instead of words that sow doubt or fear, we can remind them of their
God-given identity:

* * "You are fearfully and wonderfully made." (Psalms 139:14)

* * "You are chosen and dearly loved." (Colossians 3:12)

* "You can do all things through Christ who strengthens you." (Philippians 4:13)

By filling their hearts with God's truth, we equip them to speak that same truth into the world around them.

PRACTICAL WAYS TO TEACH YOUR CHILDREN TO SPEAK LIFE:

* **Model Life-Giving Speech:** Let your words reflect love, encouragement, and faith. Even when correcting, speak with grace and wisdom.

* **Teach the Power of Words:** Share scriptures about the impact of our words and encourage your children to think before they speak.

* **Encourage Prayer and Affirmations:** Teach them to pray over themselves and others, using words of blessing and truth.

* **Correct with Love:** Instead of harsh words, use discipline to guide and build up, pointing them back to God's grace.

* **Create a Culture of Gratitude:** Help your children develop a habit of thankfulness, speaking positively about their lives and those around them.

Activity: Speaking Life Challenge

Encourage your child to keep a "Speak Life Journal" for a week. Each day, have them write down:

A kind word they spoke to someone.

A Bible verse they used to encourage themselves or someone else.

A prayer for someone who needs uplifting.

At the weeks end, reflect together on how speaking life impacted their hearts and the people around them.

A PRAYER FOR SPEAKING LIFE

Heavenly Father,

Thank you for the power of words. Please help me to be a mother who speaks life, encouragement, and truth over my children. Let my words reflect your love and grace. Teach my children to use their tongues to glorify you, to build others up, and to declare your promises over their lives. May our home be filled with words that bring peace, joy, and faith.

In Jesus' name, Amen.

COMMUNICATION BUILDS TRUST

"Let your conversation be always full of grace, seasoned with salt, so that you may know how to answer everyone"
Colossians 4:6 NIV

Communication is the foundation of any strong relationship, and this is especially true in parenting. As mothers, we desire deep, meaningful connections with our children and relationships built on love, honesty, and trust. But trust doesn't happen automatically; it grows through open, consistent, and grace-filled communication.

God models this for us through His Word. He invites us into conversation through prayer, reassuring us that he is always listening. As our Heavenly Father desires a close relationship with us, we should cultivate a safe space where our children feel heard, understood, and valued. When we create an atmosphere of open dialogue, our children learn that they can come to us with their fears, questions, and struggles without fear of judgment or rejection.

HOW TO FOSTER COMMUNICATION THAT BUILDS TRUST:

* **Be Present & Attentive** – Set aside distractions and give your child your full attention when they speak. Show them that their words matter.

* **Listen Without Judgment** – Create a safe space for honesty by responding with grace rather than immediate

criticism or correction.

* **Encourage Open-Ended Conversations** – Instead of yes-or-no questions, ask things like, *"How did that make you feel?"* or *"What do you think would be the best way to handle this?"*

* **Model Honest & Respectful Communication** – Let your child see you practice honesty, patience, and respect in your conversations with them and others.

* **Pray Together** – Teach your child that communication with God is just as important. Encourage them to talk to God about their fears, hopes, and struggles, as they would with you.

Activity: *"Heart-to-Heart"* Journal

Start a shared journal with your child where they can write letters to you about anything on their heart—questions, worries, or just daily thoughts. Respond with encouraging words, prayers, and affirmations. This simple practice strengthens trust and provides another avenue for open communication.

A Prayer for Building Trust in Communication

Heavenly Father,

Thank you for being a God who listens. Help reflect your grace and patience in communicating with my child.

Teach me to listen with love, speak with wisdom, and create a home where my child feels safe to share their heart. Let our conversations be full of truth, encouragement, and trust, drawing us closer to each other and you.

In Jesus' name, Amen.

FINAL
REFLECTION

MIRRORS IN MOTHERHOOD: A REFLECTION FOR GRACE

"And we all, who with unveiled faces contemplate the Lord's glory, are being transformed into his image with ever-increasing glory, which comes from the Lord, who is the Spirit."
2 Corinthians 3:18 NIV

Looking at your child is like seeing your reflection in a mirror. You might not always realize how deeply your actions, words, and emotions shape your children's behavior. The struggles you carry, whether spoken or unspoken, often manifest in them. In my early stages of Motherhood, I wrestled with emotional regulation, reacting out of frustration when my children misbehaved or ignored my instructions. Over time, I saw my patterns reflected in them; the raised voices, the moments of impatience, the overwhelm in difficult situations. Their responses mirrored my own, revealing how I was not glorifying God in my actions.

Motherhood is not just about guiding our children; but also about allowing God to guide us. How we handle stress, show love, and respond to life's challenges teaches them far more than our words ever could. When I saw my children replicating my struggles, it was a wake-up call, a divine invitation to shift my heart and lean deeper into God's grace.

I encourage you to take a moment to truly look in the mirror. Not just at your physical reflection, but at the spiritual and emotional image you portray to your children. What do you see? Are there areas where

God is calling you to grow? Once you have done this, invite God into that space. Ask Him to show you how He sees you, not as a sum of your mistakes, but as His beloved child, full of potential and grace.

This journey is not just about looking but about believing; that we are being transformed through God's eyes. When we embrace his love and correction, we begin to reflect his righteousness, showing our children how to live and trust him. Even if what you see today is challenging, know that God's word is the foundation for lasting change. His love empowers us to become the mothers he designed us to be full of patience, wisdom, and unwavering grace.

Reflection Questions:

1. What areas of my life do I see reflected in my child's behavior?

2. How can I can be more intentional in modeling Christ's love and grace to my children this week?

3. Have I invited God into my struggles as a parent, or have I been trying to handle them on my own?

PRAYER: A MOTHER'S REFLECTION

Heavenly Father,

Thank you for the gift of Motherhood and how you use it to shape and refine me. As I reflect on my journey, I acknowledge the moments of joy, the struggles, and the lessons you have woven into my heart. I see how my words, actions, and even my unspoken burdens are reflected in my children, and I ask for your grace to transform me into the mother you have called me to be.

Lord, where I have been impatient, fill me with your peace. Where I have been overwhelmed, remind me that your strength is made perfect in my weakness. Where I have fallen short, cover me with your mercy and guide me to walk in love, wisdom, and grace.

Help me see myself through your eyes, not as a sum of my mistakes, but as your beloved child, ever-growing and ever-transforming in your presence. Let my life reflect your love; so my children may see you through me. May my home be filled with patience, understanding, and the unshakable foundation of faith.

I surrender my fears, shortcomings, and uncertainties to you, trusting that you are still at work in me and my children. Let my reflection glorify you, shaping my children not just by my words but by my example.

Thank you, Lord, for your endless grace and walking this journey with me. I trust you to complete the good work you have begun in me and my children.

In Jesus' name, Amen.

RESOURCES FOR MOTHERS

As mothers, we often need support, encouragement, and guidance to navigate the journey of Motherhood. Below is a list of valuable resources that help in postpartum care, maternal mental health, faith-based encouragement, parenting, and self-care. These organizations and programs offer helpful tools to uplift and support mothers in various aspects of their lives.

POSTPARTUM & MATERNAL MENTAL HEALTH SUPPORT

* **Postpartum Support International** – Provides education, advocacy, and support for mothers facing postpartum depression and anxiety.

* **Postpartum Therapy** – A resource for finding licensed therapists specializing in postpartum mental health.

* **The Motherhood Center** – Offers clinical treatment and support for perinatal mood and anxiety disorders.

* **Birth Moms Support Group** – A community for mothers needing emotional and mental health support.

* **Maternal and Child Handbook (MCHHB)** – A comprehensive maternal and child health information guide.

* **National Maternal Mental Health Hotline** – A confidential helpline for mothers seeking immediate emotional support.

* **Moms Mental Health Initiative (MMHI)** – Provides resources and peer support for moms dealing with mental health struggles.

* **Postpartum Progress** – A nonprofit organization raising awareness about postpartum depression and anxiety.

* **The Blue Dot Project** – Focuses on reducing the stigma surrounding maternal mental health conditions.

* **2020 Mom** – Dedicated to improving maternal mental health care through advocacy and education.

Faith-Based Support for Moms

* **MOPS (Mothers of Preschoolers)** – A Christian-based organization that connects and supports moms through local groups and resources.

* **Hope Mommies** – A faith-based support network for mothers who have experienced infant loss.

* **Proverbs 31 Ministries** – Provides daily encouragement and devotionals for Christian women, including support for mothers.

* **Focus on the Family - Parenting** – A Christian-based resource offering advice, articles, and encouragement.

Parenting & Family Support

* **Parenting With Love & Logic** – A research-backed approach to parenting that emphasizes empathy and responsibility.

* **National Institute of Mental Health** – Offers research and information on mental health conditions affecting parents.

* **Changes Parent Support Network (CPSN)** – A peer-led support group for parents dealing with family challenges.

* **Zero to Three** – Provides research-based guidance on early childhood development and parenting best practices.

* **Big Life Journal** – Positive mindset activities and growth mindset tools for parents and kids.

Self-Care & Wellness for Moms

* **National Maternal Mental Health Hotline** – A helpline for mothers seeking emotional and mental health support.

* **Wellness Mama** – Offers natural health and wellness tips for busy moms.

* **Mighty Moms** – A motherhood blog with practical tips on parenting, mental health, and self-care.

Motherhood is a journey that comes with both joys and challenges. It's important to seek help when needed and surround yourself with support. These resources can guide and uplift you as you navigate the beautiful yet demanding role of being a mother.

A CALL TO CONTINUE THE JOURNEY

Your journey in Motherhood is ever-unfolding. Every challenge you face, every moment of joy, and every lesson learned to shape you and your children in ways beyond what you can see. Keep embracing each day with grace, knowing that growth happens in the small quiet moments as much as in the big life-changing ones. You are not just raising your children but shaping their future with love, patience, and faith. Keep reflecting, growing, and trusting that God has equipped you for this beautiful calling. You are seen, you are loved, and you are more than enough.

Keondria Walker